Anorexia Nervosa
starving for attention

THE ENCYCLOPEDIA OF PSYCHOLOGICAL DISORDERS

Senior Consulting Editor Carol C. Nadelson, M.D.
Consulting Editor Claire E. Reinburg

Anorexia Nervosa
starving for attention

Dan Harmon

CHELSEA HOUSE PUBLISHERS
Philadelphia

The ENCYCLOPEDIA OF PSYCHOLOGICAL DISORDERS provides up-to-date information on the history of, causes and effects of, and treatment and therapies for problems affecting the human mind. The titles in this series are not intended to take the place of the professional advice of a psychiatrist or mental health care professional.

Cover Photos: Photo Researchers, Inc. NYC

Chelsea House Publishers
Editor in Chief: Stephen Reginald
Managing Editor: James D. Gallagher
Production Manager: Pamela Loos
Art Director: Sara Davis
Director of Photography: Judy L. Hasday
Senior Production Editor: Lisa Chippendale

Staff for ANOREXIA NERVOSA
Editorial Assistant: Lily Sprague
Picture Researcher: Patricia Burns
Associate Art Director: Takeshi Takahashi
Designer: Keith Trego
Cover Design: Brian Wible

The ChelseaHouse World Wide Web site address is
http://www.chelseahouse.com

Library of Congress Cataloging-in-Publication Data

Harmon, Dan.
Anorexia nervosa : starving for attention / by Dan Harmon.
    p. cm. — (The encyclopedia of psychological disorders)
Includes bibliographical references and index.
Summary: Explores the truth and misconceptions regarding
anorexia nervosa by examining its history, causes, considerations,
treatment, and related eating disorders.
ISBN 0-7910-4901-9 (hardcover)
1. Anorexia nervosa—Juvenile literature. 2. Bulimia—Juvenile literature.
3. Eating disorders—Juvenile literature. [1. Anorexia nervosa. 2. Bulimia.
3. Eating disorders.] I. Title. II. Series.
RC552.A5H38 1998
616.85'262—dc21
                                                    98-25197
                                                       CIP
2 3 4 5 6 7 8 9   AC

CONTENTS

PSYCHOLOGICAL DISORDERS AND THEIR EFFECT

CAROL C. NADELSON, M.D.
PRESIDENT AND CHIEF EXECUTIVE OFFICER,
The American Psychiatric Press

There are a wide range of problems that are considered psychological disorders, including mental and emotional disorders, problems related to alcohol and drug abuse, and some diseases that cause both emotional and physical symptoms. Psychological disorders often begin in early childhood, but during adolescence we see a sharp increase in the number of people affected by these disorders. It has been estimated that about 20 percent of the U.S. population will have some form of mental disorder sometime during their lifetime. Some psychological disorders appear following severe stress or trauma. Others appear to occur more often in some families and may have a genetic or inherited component. Still other disorders do not seem to be connected to any cause we can yet identify. There has been a great deal of attention paid to learning about the causes and treatments of these disorders, and exciting new research has taught us a great deal in the last few decades.

The fact that many new and successful treatments are available makes it especially important that we reject old prejudices and outmoded ideas that consider mental disorders to be untreatable. If psychological problems are identified early, it is possible to prevent serious consequences. We should not keep these problems hidden or feel shame that we or a member of our family has a mental disorder. Some people believe that something they said or did caused a mental disorder. Some people think that these disorders are "only in your head" so that you could "snap out of it" if you made the effort. This type of thinking implies that a treatment is a matter of willpower or motivation. It is a terrible burden for someone who is suffering to be blamed for their misery, and often people with psychological disorders are not treated compassionately. We hope that the information in this book will teach you about various mental illnesses.

The problems covered in the volumes in the ENCYCLOPEDIA OF PSYCHOLOGICAL DISORDERS were selected because they are of particular importance to young adults, because they affect them directly or because they affect family and friends. There are individual volumes on reading disorders, attention deficit and disruptive behavior disorders, and dementia—all of these are related to our abilities to learn and integrate information from the world around us. There are books on drug abuse that provide useful information about the effects of these drugs and treatments that are available for those individuals who have drug problems. Some of the books concentrate on one of the most common mental disorders, depression. Others deal with eating disorders, which are dangerous illnesses that affect a large number of young adults, especially women.

Most of the public attention paid to these disorders arises from a particular incident involving a celebrity that awakens us to our own vulnerability to psychological problems. These incidents of celebrities or public figures revealing their own psychological problems can also enable us to think about what we can do to prevent and treat these types of problems.

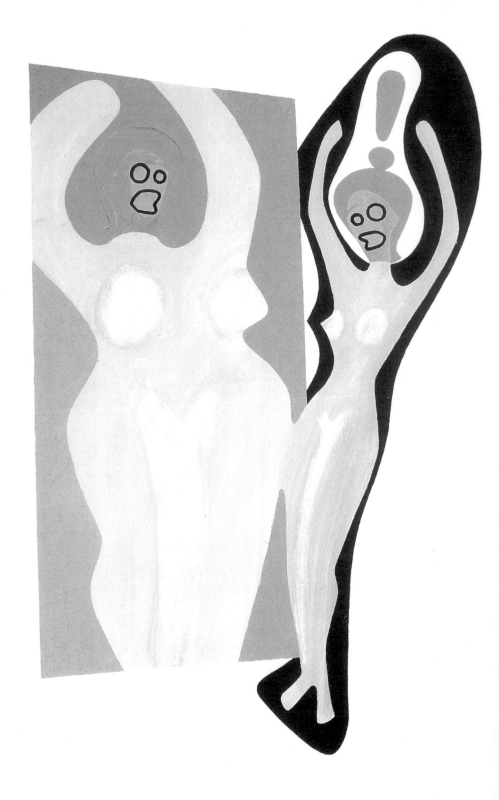

ANOREXIA NERVOSA: AN OVERVIEW

Anorexia nervosa is an eating disorder that can cause a person to literally "waste away," in some cases starving to death. Anorexics develop an intense fear of gaining weight and perceive themselves as fat even when they are, in reality, rail-thin. They may try to stop eating entirely, exercise excessively, or purge their food by vomiting or misusing laxatives. The malnutrition caused by these extreme techniques can cause irreparable damage to the anorexic's body, even if the disease is treated before it kills.

There are several other disorders that are often found together with anorexia, including bulimia nervosa, an eating disorder characterized by repeated episodes of overeating, or "binging," and then purging the food. Bulimia is thought to be more common than anorexia, and can have many of the same effects, as well as a few others that are caused by the frequent purging process. Depression may also appear with anorexia or bulimia, contributing to the person's desire not to eat and making treatment more difficult.

Most often, eating disorders affect teenage girls and young women; females are estimated to be seven to ten times more likely to develop an eating disorder than males. Further risk factors include family life (anorexics often come from families where there are strict rules or rigid expectations, or where there are problems in the home), genetic predisposition (if others in the family have also suffered from eating disorders), and chemical imbalances in the parts of the brain that control metabolism and reaction to stress.

This book will discuss the symptoms, history, and causes of anorexia, and will explain how to get help for someone who appears to have the disease, as well as how to confront the problem if you think you may have anorexia yourself. The sooner an eating disorder is recognized and treated, the less likely it is to cause lasting damage, and the more likely it is that the person suffering from it can successfully return to a normal, healthy life.

Singer Karen Carpenter, with her brother Richard, during her battle with anorexia nervosa. Karen died in 1983 of heart failure brought on by her self-starvation.

1

DEATH OF A SINGER

"I'm on the top of the world. . . ."

Karen Carpenter gaily sang those words in a hit song she recorded with her older brother, Richard. It was one of their many famous songs. The Carpenters had four top-five hits in 1969, their first year with a national recording company. Throughout most of the 1970s, they were among the best-selling recording artists on the planet. Seventeen of their singles made Billboard's Top 20. Indeed, for almost a decade, it was a rare moment when one or more of their songs was not on the charts. Eventually, they would sell an unbelievable 100 million records!

In the world of entertainment, the Carpenters truly reached "the top" very quickly. And they stayed there a long time. Undreamed-of popularity, constant travel around the globe, adoring audiences—this was the lifestyle of Karen and Richard Carpenter. They were so successful they both could have retired while still in their twenties and lived very well the rest of their lives. But why stop? Karen was doing what she enjoyed most: singing and playing the drums. No other vocalist in the world had a voice to match hers. Few entertainers would ever attain the pinnacle of success she and her brother had.

Yet unknown to her fans, Karen had a terrible problem. She was worried about her weight. Overly worried. After a reporter made an unflattering reference to her figure, she began taking drastic measures to stay slim. In fact, she took measures that jeopardized her health. No one who looked at her would ever have considered her to be "fat" at all. But she saw herself quite differently. She began starving herself. She would take laxatives and make herself vomit to avoid storing fat. A good meal, to Karen, consisted of tea and a salad. Once her weight obsession began, she found she could not control it. Weakened, she became unable to perform as she once did.

Karen was only 32 years old when she died in February 1983. The immediate cause of death was heart failure. But what brought this on? Some thought stardom had brought about Karen's death—at least indirectly. True, the touring schedule had been exhausting. When you are a star, there is pressure to live up to your own image, to please your fans. For Karen, the demands of her career, combined with the worsening of her physical condition, were so taxing she had been forced to take a break from performing for more than a year before her death.

But that wasn't the whole story. Karen suffered from a lethal combination of sinister and complex diseases called anorexia nervosa and bulimia. The pressures of jobs, relationships, and various other life situations can serve to "drive" these illnesses. Yet even after she had suspended her music career, Karen found the problem more than she could manage. As one expert points out, "You can't beat anorexia with an hour in a doctor's office." Karen had struggled to cope not just for an hour, but for more than seven years.

WHAT IS ANOREXIA?

Anorexia nervosa is a type of eating disorder. It is categorized as a psychological disorder, not merely a physical abnormality. A short, basic definition of anorexia nervosa has been outlined by Dr. W. Stewart Agras, who describes it as "a relatively rare disorder characterized by marked weight loss (at least 15 percent below ideal body weight), an intense fear of gaining weight, disturbance in the experience of body shape (i.e., feeling fat in the face of marked weight loss), and (in females) amenorrhea [lack of menstruation]" (Agras, 1995).

Anorexic persons do not eat properly. They honestly believe they are doing the correct thing by refusing to do so. They insist on undereating because a normal diet is, to them, overeating.

Usually the anorexic episode starts with simple dieting. But the preoccupation with weight control takes on unusual dimensions. Anorexics don't avoid just fatty foods. Many anorexics count calories—literally. They carefully measure every ounce of food and liquid before consuming it. They religiously watch their scale. If the needle exceeds their desired mark, they take immediate measures to lose a pound (or two, for good measure). To make sure it doesn't happen again, they may lower their weight goal. Over time, their desired weight then drops below the danger zone, and their actual weight soon follows. At the same time,

Often, anorexia begins with a period of dieting. The anorexic then begins to feel unable or unwilling to stop dieting, despite dangerous weight loss.

anorexics may put themselves through grueling and potentially harmful exercise regimens.

THE PHYSICAL CONSEQUNECES

The results of anorexia nervosa are terrible to witness. Some of the signs are obvious to everyone; others can be concealed by the anorexic. They may include many or all of these:

- Muscle tissue becomes wasted.
- The skin may appear jaundiced (yellowish) and rough. A silky sheen of hair may grow on the cheeks and other parts of the body.
- Calcium can be lost, leading to potential bone problems.
- The person can suffer from constipation, dry skin, brittle fingernails, swelling of the joints, and bodily soreness.

Anorexia is often a product of a distorted body image. Despite what the mirror shows, an anorexic who is severely underweight will still complain of being fat.

- Blood pressure can become erratic. The pulse rate can drop to as low as 60 heartbeats per minute while the person is awake, 30 beats per minute while asleep. This can lead to problems with the heart, such as heart murmurs, or even to a change in heart size.
- Anemia, an unhealthy reduction of red blood cells, is common. This can cause feelings of tiredness and other unpleasant effects.
- Anorexics commonly complain of feeling cold; their core body temperature may be as low as 93 degrees Fahrenheit (98.6 degrees is the normal temperature).
- Extreme starvation can alter the physical construction of the brain. For instance, the spaces containing cerebrospinal fluid can be enlarged.
- The sense of taste changes: salty foods and hot spices become less perceptible.

Even after these symptoms are exhibited, the condition deteriorates further. Sleep irregularity, feelings of despair, and kidney problems may develop. Vomiting and the abuse of laxatives can upset the body's electrolyte balance (levels of salts, acids, and other components) (Casper, 1995).

Once these unhealthy symptoms begin, they become self-perpetuating. For example, as certain foods lose their taste, the person is less likely to be excited by food, thereby making it easier to abstain from eating. Also, a lowered body temperature can, in turn, affect the heart rate (Casper, 1995). Finally, if it goes untreated, anorexia nervosa can progress to one final, tragic result: death.

For a few people, mealtime is an unpleasant experience. They pick at their food, reluctant to eat, anxious for the "meal ordeal" to be over.

2

WHAT, EXACTLY, IS THE PROBLEM?

Most of us love to eat. Some of the happiest moments of our day are mealtimes. Hungry students bounding down the hall to the cafeteria are hard to contain because they are excited about where they are going (even though they may complain about cafeteria food). Almost without exception, couples and families being seated at a restaurant table are beaming with anticipation, not scowling with dread.

But for a few, "food" is a bad word. Mealtime is a period of stress. These individuals pick over their plates reluctantly, aware that they are out of sync with those around them. They can't wait for the meal ordeal to end.

It's certainly not unusual for people to be weight conscious. In Western societies, broadcast and print media (especially in commercials and advertisements) glamorize people with slender bodies. People who see thin models naturally want their own bodies to look that way. As a result almost everybody diets at some time.

The *Harvard Medical School Mental Health Letter* reports that more than half the women in the country are dieting (Dec. 1992–Jan. 1993). That may be okay because Americans tend to be overweight. But dieting must be undertaken with great care because it can also be destructive. The *Letter* observes, "The more intense the social pressure for slimness, the more likely it is that a troubled girl or young woman will develop an eating disorder rather than some other psychiatric symptom—especially if she also regards self-control in eating as a sign of the discipline needed for high achievement and social success."

It would be grossly simplistic to call anorexia nervosa a preoccupation with dieting. The definitive *Diagnostic and Statistical Manual of Mental Disorders,* (*DSM-IV*), in its overview of this complex disorder, signals a much more ominous situation: "The essential features of anorexia nervosa are that the individual refuses to maintain a minimally normal body weight, is intensely afraid of gaining weight, and exhibits a significant disturbance in the perception of the shape or size of his or her body."

Ironically, as the *DSM-IV* points out, the use of the word "anorexia" in labeling this disease is inaccurate. "Anorexia" means "a loss of appetite." People suffering from anorexia nervosa, however, typically do not lose their appetites; they become hungry like everyone else. Instead, they discipline themselves to overcome their appetites. Dieting requires discipline, and in this regard, anorexics are indeed "successful" dieters. They are extremely successful—dangerously so.

It is estimated that one in 100 preteen and teenage girls (the gender and age group most at risk) will fall victim to anorexia nervosa. And one in 10 of these individuals will die from its effects: sheer starvation, heart failure, or suicide due to severe depression, which often accompanies the disease, says the *DSM-IV*. Two researchers, Dr. Wayne A. Bowers and Dr. Arnold E. Andersen, suggest that the rates are higher and that the eventual death rate from anorexia-related causes may be as high as one in five.

THREE CASE STUDIES

In the opening chapter you read the story of Karen Carpenter, probably the most famous victim of anorexia nervosa. To understand better the nature of this fearful disease, let's look at three more case studies (the names are fictitious):

Jamie was 16 when a boy at school joked that she wouldn't be invited to a dance because she was too fat. Jamie wasn't fat—she weighed 110 pounds. But she believed him and decided to go on a diet.

A simple way to reduce, she reasoned, was simply to skip lunch. But this didn't result in fast enough weight loss, so she began skipping breakfast too. And when she did eat, she would carefully weigh the food first.

These measures worked: She lost 17 pounds in a matter of months. In her mind, she was achieving a figure like those of the swimsuit models she envied. But she was far from happy and healthy. Her joints and fingers were swollen; split ends in her hair, always an annoyance, became a nightmare; her fingernails frequently broke. And she still considered herself fat.

An alarming incident saved Jamie. She passed out from weakness one

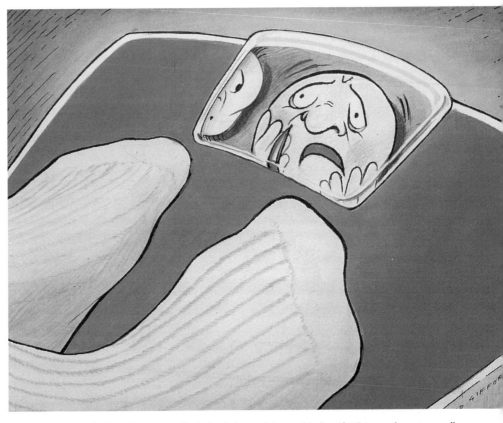

Anorexics, especially females, are terrified of gaining weight or of being "fat." Anorexics set unrealistic "ideal" weights that are far below normal.

day as she boarded a bus. When she was taken to a hospital, the doctor suspected that she had anorexia nervosa. She was hospitalized, and treatment began.

■   ■   ■

Belinda was the same age as Jamie. She might have been considered overweight, but only by a few pounds. Belinda was attractive and courteous and was an excellent student. It bothered her that she didn't have a boyfriend. When her father suggested she needed to lose some weight if she wanted to get a date, Belinda began dieting. She lost several pounds. Propelled by her success, she decided to go for a completely new look, and her diet became the most important thing in her life.

To those around her, it was obvious Belinda was becoming seriously

Frequently an anorexic will count calories, keeping a careful total, or weigh and measure all the food that he or she eats in order to "ration" it.

underweight. Yet she continued to watch the scale like a hawk. She cut her food into tiny fragments and weighed them and measured out her milk, juice, and soda. She placed the items in little containers and stored them neatly. These were her "rations."

She began to spend much of her time exercising. She would always take the stairs, avoiding elevators. She would do countless knee bends and sit-ups.

As her weight dropped and her body became weak, her menstrual periods stopped. Still she did not acknowledge that she had a dreadful problem, and none of her friends or family could persuade her that she did. Finally, her family doctor ordered her to be hospitalized. Even after therapy began, she didn't believe she was really sick.

Over time, Belinda had to be readmitted to the hospital for several terms of inpatient care. Finally, she could no longer deny that her attitude toward weight control and physical health was unnatural and unrealistic. Only then did she begin to make progress in combating the illness.

■　　　■　　　■

Sam was 14 when his front teeth were hurt in an accident. His parents found it hard to get him to eat; he protested that biting and chewing caused too much pain. Over a six-month period, his weight dropped by a third.

At first Sam had a logical excuse for not wanting to eat. However, after his mouth injury healed, Sam did not resume a normal diet. He claimed his stomach felt bloated if he ate a full meal and especially if he ate sweets. He began insisting that his mother prepare foods with a low oil content.

Sam combined extensive exercise with this austere diet, which made him very thin, but not strong. On the contrary, he was constantly fatigued, irritable, constipated, and cold. He became so weak he couldn't go to school. When he couldn't even lift his arms, his parents took him to the hospital.

Sam had been overweight when he was younger. Schoolmates had called him "fat boy." But he insisted this had never bothered him and was not the reason he now ate so little. After several months in the hospital, Sam regained most of his normal weight and became strong again. Once dismissed, though, he began losing weight so rapidly that he had to be readmitted to the hospital. Upon his release, he was able to keep himself relatively healthy. But he relied on snacks rather than full meals to keep his weight at a level considered acceptable for his height (Lai et al., 1995).

■　　　■　　　■

It's interesting to note that in three of this book's examples (Karen Carpenter, Jamie, and Belinda), it was a passing comment about being overweight that set the disease in motion. Anorexics are often individuals who believe they must live up to the expectations of others. They tend to be obedient and well-disciplined.

This extreme dieting behavior can also be caused when a young girl looks in the mirror and discovers that she is beginning puberty and her body is starting to change. It may also be caused by a traumatic life event, such as a death in the family or of a close friend, parental divorce, or breaking up with a boyfriend. Often, a new diet is timed to coincide with a point of change, such as beginning college or starting at a new school, because the anorexic believes that he or she will be more readily accepted if thin.

In the next section we look at some other common characteristics of anorexics.

PROFILE OF THE ANOREXIC

Generally, anorexia nervosa is considered to be a disease most likely to strike teenage girls and young women. Certainly the great majority of anorexics—possibly as many as 95 percent—are female. However, males, too, can be anorexic. There is also some evidence that many anorexics may be older adults, and some researchers have speculated that there are two kinds of anorexia, one involving younger people and the other afflicting older people (Gagnon, 1996). But according to the *DSM-IV*, "the mean age at onset for anorexia nervosa is 17 years, with some data suggesting bimodal peaks at ages 14 and 18 years. The onset of this disorder rarely occurs in females over age 40 years."

Most cases seem to be found in Western cultures, notably in Europe and the United States. They are thought to be more common among middle- and upper-class families than among the poor and more common among whites than among other races. Also, as recorded by the *DSM-IV*, "anorexia nervosa appears to be far more prevalent in industrialized societies, in which there is an abundance of food and in which, especially for females, being considered attractive is linked to being thin."

Anorexic children, for the most part, are models of good behavior. They tend to be good students and sometimes they are perfectionists. Not surprisingly, in cases involving adults, the individuals are usually successful at what they do. Studies noted in the *Harvard Medical School Mental Health Letter* reveal that American women who are highly educated and well-to-do are usually in control of their weight (Dec.

DEATH OF A DANCER

Members of the Boston Ballet company gather at a press conference to discuss the death of dancer Heidi Guenther on June 30, 1997. Guenther was 5'3" and weighed only 100 pounds when she died suddenly while on vacation with her family. Coroners were unable to determine a specific cause of death; specialists say that people with severe anorexia often die of heart arrhythmias that are not detected in autopsies.

Guenther had been a rising star with the Boston Ballet when she was told by an assistant artistic director that in order to dance principal roles, she would need to lose weight. Friends became concerned by her weight loss in the next few months, and Guenther's mother worried about how thin she looked at Christmas. When the company took its summer break, the now rail-thin Guenther was told to gain back some of the lost weight. Sadly, she died before she had the chance.

Insomnia is a common problem for anorexics, along with fear of inferiority, social withdrawal, moodiness, and depression.

1992–Jan. 1993). Unhappily, for some, weight control becomes an obsession . . . and worse.

Anorexics tend to be good athletes and dancers. In fact, a young woman may begin running or another sport, enjoy losing weight, and like this new thinness so much that she decides to stop eating altogether. Once this person becomes anorexic, exercise remains a vital part of their lives—but for the wrong reason. They often overexercise in order to continue losing weight (*Harvard*, Dec. 1992–Jan. 1993). They will get up early in the morning to work out before the rest of the family gets up, then work out again in the afternoon or evening. All of this activity, compounded by the lack of sleep and eating that accompanies it, reflects the anorexic's desire to subjugate their body into "perfect" thinness.

What may be surprising is that many anorexics have an uncommon knowledge of and interest in food. Strangely, although they refuse to eat, they may be recipe collectors and even gourmet cooks who serve elaborate meals to their family and friends.

While the anorexic person's weight loss is obvious, he or she may seem to eat normally. The person may eat a lot of salads and fruits, for example. Whereas these foods can constitute a lot of forkfuls, they carry too few calories by themselves to sustain a healthy body (Royal College of Psychiatrists leaflet).

The anorexic will find other ways to avoid eating. He or she may often be late in the morning and miss breakfast, join sports activities at school and miss lunch, and make excuses for not attending family meals. If this person does eat with others, he or she will pick at the food, push it around the plate so that it looks as if it has been eaten, or take tiny bites of a low-calorie food such as an apple or a piece of lettuce, chewing it hundreds of times to delay swallowing. Because most anorexics do not like the feeling of having food in their stomach, they avoid drinking anything—even water—because it will cause a sensation of fullness.

A CATASTROPHIC LIFESTYLE

Regardless of the severity, anorexia nervosa results in a dysfunctional life. Because of their emaciated condition, anorexics commonly suffer from such problems as the following, which can have an unpleasant and even harmful impact on people around them:

- Bad mood (sometimes even clinical depression)
- Irritable nature
- Shyness or introversion, to the point of social withdrawal
- Fear of inferiority
- Sleeping problems
- Obsessive-compulsive tendencies
- Loss of interest in sex

It is not unusual to find that anorexics experience compulsions and even addictions to many things, from drugs and gambling to schoolwork and sex. Other associated symptoms might be feelings of guilt or anxiety.

Physically, malnourishment can lead to complications with the vital organs, including the heart and liver. Slowed heartbeats and breathing rates occur. The person may be more susceptible to colds and other sicknesses. Also, if he or she engages in forced vomiting, the acid over time can damage tooth enamel.

THE *DSM-IV*'S DEFINITION

The first criterion for diagnosing anorexia nervosa is that "the individual maintains a body weight that is below a minimally normal level for age and height." In the case of a child, it may be that the youth does not lose weight but fails, over time, to keep pace with peers in bodily growth.

At what point, exactly, is a person officially considered to be underweight and possibly anorexic? The *DSM-IV* identifies the threshold as less than 85 percent of the normal weight. This means that the person is at least 15 percent below normal weight. Of course, this is only a guideline: "It is unreasonable to specify a single standard for minimally normal weight that applies to all individuals of a given age and height," notes the DSM-IV. In determining a minimally normal weight, the clinician should consider not only such guidelines but also the individual's body build and weight history.

The second criterion is that the person not only be unnaturally weight conscious but actually have an "intense fear" of gaining weight. In fact, the anorexic may become more concerned about weight gain even as his or her actual weight continues to decrease.

Third, "the experience and significance of body weight and shape are distorted in these individuals. Some individuals feel globally overweight [fat in every part of the body]. Others realize that they are thin, but are still concerned that certain parts of their bodies, particularly the abdomen, buttocks, and thighs, are 'too fat.' They may employ a wide variety of techniques to estimate their body size or weight, including excessive weighing, obsessive measuring of body parts, and persistently using a mirror to check for perceived areas of 'fat.'"

Weight and figure largely determine the anorexic person's self-esteem. If he or she remains thin, it's seen as an impressive achievement. Weight gain—even normal weight gain—is considered failure.

A fourth criterion for females is the absence of menstruation (or, in the case of preteenage girls, a delay in the development of menses). In some anorexic women, menstruation actually stops before their weight drops drastically (*Harvard*, Dec. 1992–Jan 1993). This can cause long-term problems with childbearing and can also affect the person's calcium level, which leads to bone-related ailments. Correspondingly, anorexic men are often sexually impotent.

The *DSM-IV* indicates that it is rare for an individual with anorexia nervosa to complain about weight loss. Thus it's unlikely the person will

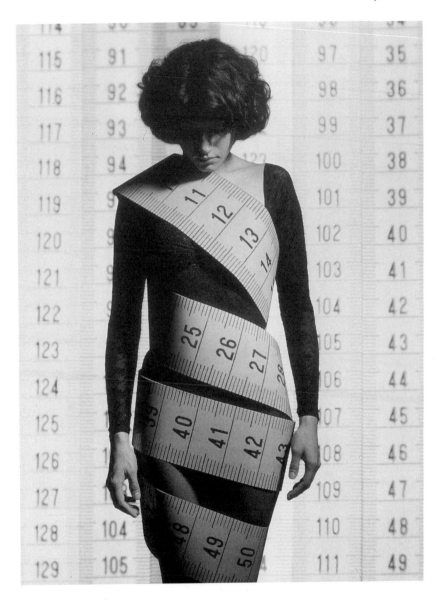

The anorexic's self-esteem is entirely dependent on weight and figure. Losing weight, the anorexic believes, is the way to become more attractive and more perfect.

seek help voluntarily. In most cases, family members must insist on medical attention. And doctors know they usually cannot expect a realistic self-evaluation or a completely truthful statement of case history in the initial interview of an anorexic person.

Television star Oprah Winfrey, whose public cycle of weight gain and loss through various diets is an example of Western culture's fascination with thinness.

SUBTYPES DIFFER IN SEVERITY

It should be noted that not all anorexics behave identically in their approach to weight control. Some act more radically than others.

There are two subtypes of the disease. The less severe subtype is known as the restricting type. Persons in this category seek to maintain their weight level simply by strict dieting or fasting, usually coupled with intense exercise.

Those who behave more radically are of the binge-eating/purging type. In these cases, the individuals don't merely fast and exercise, they take more extreme and immediate measures to eliminate weight. Often they satisfy their hunger by binge eating. Then they immediately "purge" by making themselves vomit or by taking laxatives and fluid eliminators and even by using enemas. While it appears that most individuals with binge-eating/purging type engage in these behaviors at least weekly, there is not enough information to know the minimum frequency of purging (*DSM-IV*).

IS OUR DEFINITION ACCURATE?

It seems the more research that is conducted, the less sure psychologists are of the precise nature of anorexia nervosa. Some investigators, for instance, are scrutinizing the real impact of the criterion of "weight phobia." According to the medical definition, a person must demonstrate a fear of gaining weight in order to warrant a diagnosis of anorexia nervosa. But a 1993 report in the *American Journal of Psychiatry* questioned the weight phobia factor.

The researchers pointed out that until about 1930, psychologists did not consider the fear of gaining weight to be a predominant motive in a person's rejection of food. And how should we diagnose cases of deliberate starvation when the element of fear is apparently not a root cause? The researchers noted that in India and Hong Kong, for instance, "weight phobia is absent in many anorexic patients."

To arrive at an answer these researchers suggested three possible scenarios:

1. A person who exhibits many or most anorexic symptoms except weight phobia may be diagnosed as having an eating disorder not otherwise specified—not anorexia nervosa.

2. The person in question may be afraid of gaining weight but may be able to conceal this fear from examiners.

3. Over decades of study, the psychological/medical community has witnessed "a transformation in the content" of the disorder.

Their original question: Would anorexia nervosa be the same illness if the criterion of weight phobia were not required? And their answer: The disorder "may be conceptualized in several different ways without including the phenomenon of weight phobia or body image disturbance." Of course, this means changing the established definition of anorexia nervosa. The researchers observed that further careful study of intentional starvation outside the United States and Europe can help

DIAGNOSIS CRITERIA FOR ANOREXIA NERVOSA

Diagnosis Criteria for Anorexia Nervosa

A. Refusal to maintain body weight at or above a minimally normal weight for age and height (e.g., weight loss leading to maintenance of body weight less than 85 percent of that expected; or failure to make expected weight gain during period of growth, leading to body weight gain less than 85 percent of that expected).

B. Intense fear of gaining weight or becoming fat, even though underweight.

C. Disturbance in the way in which one's body weight or shape is experienced, undue influence of body weight or shape on self-evaluation, or denial of the seriousness of the current low body weight.

D. In postmenarcheal females, amenorrhea, i.e., the absence of at least three consecutive menstrual cycles. (A woman is considered to have amenorrhea if her periods occur only following hormone, e.g., estrogen, administration.)

Specific types:

Restricting Type: during the current episode of anorexia nervosa, the person has not regularly engaged in binge-eating or purging behavior (i.e., self-induced vomiting or the misuse of laxatives, diuretics, or enemas).

Binge-Eating/Purging Type: during the current episode of anorexia nervosa, the person has regularly engaged in binge-eating or purging behavior (i.e., self-induced vomiting or the misuse of laxatives, diuretics, or enemas).

Source: *Diagnostic and Statistical Manual of Mental Disorders*, fourth edition (*DSM-IV*)

clarify the core features of the disorder. In some foreign cultures, food is less abundant, overeating is less common, and thus weight phobia would be more clearly apparent. "The influence of cultural factors (e.g., an emphasis on slimness) on the form and content of anorexia nervosa may become clarified" (Hsu and Lee, 1993).

Anorexia nervosa is often accompanied by other mental disorders. We'll learn more about those in Chapter 4. In the next chapter we look at what is known of the history of the disorder.

In 1880, the beauty standard for women called for them to be heavier than today. Here, a woman consults a doctor for a "fattening cure."

3

HISTORY
OF THE DISEASE

Our preoccupation with slimness has been described as a specifically modern concern (*Harvard*, Dec. 1992–Jan. 1993). Certainly some older generations regarded plumpness as a sign of good health. It was the death of Karen Carpenter that introduced a new term into the vocabulary of many people. Although anorexia nervosa was new to many fans shocked by the tragedy, this disorder was not new to the medical and psychological professions. The syndrome has been recognized by doctors and researchers for more than a century and was first reported about 300 years ago (Bowers and Andersen, 1995). In fact, what may have been an instance of anorexia was recorded 1,100 years ago (*Harvard*, Dec. 1992–Jan. 1993).

In the past, songs and biographies did not tell of people suffering or dying specifically from anorexia nervosa. But various folk songs have been written about "lovesick" people who were said to have died because their "hearts were broken." How many of these tragic figures were overweight—or thought they were—and plunged themselves into catastrophic cycles of weight control that today would be recognized as symptomatic of anorexia? There is no way even to guess, since the ballads and legends rarely record a victim's physical appearance. The rejected person "wasted away. . . ." That's all we know.

TALE OF A PRINCESS

An interesting story is the record of Margaret, Princess of Hungary, during the 13th century. Her father, King Bela, faced a crisis. Tartars, tribes of pillaging Mongols, were invading much of central Europe and Russia. This fearsome "Golden Horde," as they were called, were overrunning his kingdom. King Bela made a solemn pledge to God: If He would preserve his country in this

By the 1920s, thin was in. La-Mar reducing soap, like the miracle creams sold today, was supposed to melt the fat away from the body where it was applied.

dark time, he would give his daughter into the Lord's service as a nun. And that's exactly what happened.

A convent was built for Margaret on an island in the Danube River near Budapest. Did the king's daughter have a say in the matter? Not in those days—but it hardly seems to be an issue, because Margaret seemed destined for this role. She performed exhausting, undignified chores every day without complaining, perhaps even carrying her difficult responsibilities to extremes. As was the custom in convents, she fasted periodically and rose early each day to begin her work, from which she rarely rested. She was an excellent student, mastering both the Hungarian language and Latin. She would serve meals to the other nuns, then quietly retreat to pray alone rather than join them to eat.

Then the king decided Margaret should marry. He presented many royal young men to her as prospective husbands. She could have left her life of toil and become a pampered princess. But she would have nothing to do with the idea. She starved herself and neglected to wash. With a thin, emaciated body, she caught a fever and died; she was only 28 years old. Historians today suspect Margaret may have been anorexic. It is almost certain that she had a form of eating disorder (*American Journal of Psychiatry*, August 1994).

CRUDE TREATMENT

Medical diagnoses and treatments in ancient times were very primitive by modern standards. Home remedies were the only treatments commonly available. If these remedies failed to cure a serious intestinal disorder, for example, then the unhappy person's health could deteriorate quickly. The result might well be fatal. At the same time, a mentally disturbed person might be committing suicide gradually by deliberate starvation. In either case, the exact cause of death would be unknown. Both persons were said to have "wasted away and died" as far as anyone could tell. Reading their brief obituaries and tombstone epitaphs is the only record we have.

Fasting was more common in bygone ages than it is today. Often, it was a religious practice. Is there a connection between fasting and what today would be recognized as anorexia nervosa? One study suggests that, like Margaret, possibly half of the Catholic female saints of the late Middle Ages could have been anorexic. It is thought that after the Catholic Church began to emphasize the importance of good deeds

These photos of Crown Princess Victoria of Sweden highlight the physical effects of anorexia nervosa. The picture at left was taken in April 1996; the one on the right is from November 1997. After the later appearance, the royal family admitted that Victoria was struggling with an eating disorder.

rather than self-punishment and deprivation, severe fasting and its related health problems diminished among nuns and monks (*Harvard*, Dec. 1992–Jan. 1993). At least one analyst has noted the similarity between today's anorexics and yesteryear's saints (*American Journal of Psychiatry*, August 1994).

SIFTING THROUGH THE SYMPTOMS

A century ago some psychoanalysts believed anorexia nervosa was a variation of Simmonds' disease, whose symptoms are caused by problems with the body's pituitary functions. Eventually, they realized the pituitary mechanism was not necessarily damaged in anorexics (Dare, 1995).

In recent decades, anorexia nervosa has come under increasing study. Various treatments have been tried, and doctors have learned that certain other ailments often accompany the disorder. In fact, sorting out the symptoms and identifying the correct underlying illness is no simple task. By learning the exact nature of a person's disorder, doctors and therapists are better able to perform effective treatment.

Lynda Carter and Katie Wright as a single mother and her anorexic daughter in the NBC movie A Secret Between Friends. *The film deals with anorexia as well as another eating disorder, bulimia, that often occurs with anorexia.*

4

RELATED DISEASES

BULIMIA NERVOSA: THE OTHER EATING DISORDER

Bulimia nervosa is much "newer" than anorexia—at least in terms of being recognized as a distinct medical disorder. Although a record of a possible bulimic case dates as far back as the second century, it was not until the 1970s that doctors began considering it as a disease distinct from anorexia. It became known as bulimia nervosa in 1987 (*Harvard*, Dec. 1992–Jan. 1993).

The disorder tends to develop in people who are a few years older than the average anorexia nervosa patient. It is believed to be two or three times more common than anorexia. As many as 10 percent of American women may experience bulimia at some point in life (*Harvard*, Dec. 1992–Jan. 1993).

In order to be diagnosed as bulimic, a person must have indulged in at least two episodes a week of binging, followed by purging, for three months or longer. "Binging" is the frenzied eating of a great deal of food at once. "Purging" is getting rid of it quickly, before the body processes it. Pushing one's fingers down the throat to induce vomiting is an immediate form of purging. Taking laxatives is another. (The use of laxatives, by the way, is a serious practice for anyone, because repeated use can make one laxative-dependent.)

How are anorexia nervosa and bulimia nervosa different? The *DSM-IV* explains: "In bulimia nervosa, individuals exhibit recurrent episodes of binge eating, engage in inappropriate behavior to avoid weight gain (e.g., self-induced vomiting), and are overly concerned with body shape and weight." Unlike anorexics, people who have bulimia nervosa can keep their weight at or near the normal level for their height and age. Anorexics, because of their distorted ideas concerning "ideal weight," cannot.

Bulimics don't have the discipline typical of anorexics. They often diet and

The two stages of bulimia, binging and purging. A bulimic will often (at least twice a week) binge, or grossly overeat, and then purge all of the food by forced vomiting or laxative abuse before the body can process it.

exercise, as do anorexics. But rather than sticking diligently to their program, they periodically let themselves go to the opposite extreme, gorging on food. They then feel guilty and want to make amends for their overindulgence, and they disgorge. "Enjoy all the cake you want—then get rid of it." That's the simple theory, but in practice, it's not such fun. Bulimics can experience a radical weight increase and/or decrease of as much as 10 pounds during one episode. This places complex stresses on the body.

Although not as often fatal as anorexia, bulimia has many of the same unpleasant effects: weakness and soreness, for example. Ruined teeth, caused by the acid of frequent vomiting, is also not uncommon. Bulim-

THE STARVATION DIET

Tracey Gold seemed to have everything going for her. She was a pretty girl with a loving family and a role on the popular sitcom *Growing Pains*. However, she also had multiple bouts of anorexia, dropping her weight at one point to a precarious 79 pounds.

Tracey's first encounter with the disease happened when she was only 12 years old. Her pediatrician diagnosed her as anorexic, and after four months of psychiatric treatment, she seemed to have recovered fully. It was not until she was 19 that her anorexia would return.

When Tracey was 19, she decided that she wanted to lose some weight, feeling insecure about her appearance. A diet plan was drawn up for her, allotting a mere 500 calories per day (most dieticians now will not recommend eating less than 1200 calories per day, even for the most serious dieter), to allow her to lose 20 pounds and reach her "ideal weight". But the ideal came and went, and Tracey kept dieting, despite beginning psychotherapy in the spring of 1990. Two years later, at a weight of 90 pounds, she left her acting job to check into a hospital. She appeared to rebound, with the help of a nutritionist/therapist team, only to relapse a few months later and drop below 80 pounds before finally recovering enough to resume her acting career.

After her return, Tracey took on the role of an anorexic woman in the 1994 movie *For the Love of Nancy*, based on the true experiences of another anorexia sufferer, Nancy Walsh. She also spoke publicly about her illness, granting interviews to *People* magazine in 1992 in the midst of her struggle, and again in 1994 to share her triumph. Her case has helped to send a positive message to people struggling with anorexia, a message that they can overcome the disease.

ics also face possible dehydration and ruptured esophagi (*Harvard*, Dec. 1992–Jan. 1993).

It is possible for a person to suffer from both anorexia and bulimia. It's estimated that approximately half of the people who are anorexic are also bulimic. Bulimia, in fact, sometimes develops in persons who have battled anorexia for some time (Royal College of Psychiatrists leaflet). Persons suffering from both illnesses tend to be more depressed and suicidal. Depression, with such results as alcohol abuse, is especially common among bulimic anorexics.

DEPRESSION

Depression is often associated with anorexia nervosa. The depression can usually be treated, at least to some extent, with antidepressant drugs. And solving or reducing the person's depressed condition can be a significant step in the overall fight to restore the anorexic to health and happiness. If it is not treated, on the other hand, depression coupled with anorexia can form a vicious cycle: starvation, binging, and purging can heighten depression, which, in turn, may lead to renewed eating abnormalities (*Harvard*, Dec. 1992–Jan. 1993).

Psychiatrists have found that some anorexics exhibit obsessive-compulsive behavior. Some may also be impulsive, especially if they are suffering from the binge-eating/purging type of anorexia described in Chapter 2 (Bowers and Andersen, 1995).

It is important to realize that these kinds of symptoms don't necessarily mean a person is anorexic, even when coupled with drastic weight loss. For example, both depression and severe weight loss are common in cancer and AIDS patients. But "individuals with such disorders usually do not have a distorted body image and a desire for further weight loss" (*DSM-IV*).

Schizophrenics (who, like anorexics, have distorted ideas of reality, but with different symptoms and results) sometimes engage in erratic eating habits and consequently lose a lot of weight. But again, as the *DSM-IV* explains, "they rarely show the fear of gaining weight and the body image disturbance required for a diagnosis of anorexia nervosa."

Although "fear of gaining weight" is a factor that distinguishes anorexics from people who suffer from other psychological disorders with similar symptoms, it's not conclusive proof of anorexia. In explaining some of the differences between anorexia nervosa and similar illnesses, the *DSM-IV* gives us an idea of how complex is the task of correct diagnosis:

> Specifically, individuals may be humiliated or embarrassed to be seen eating in public, as in Social Phobia; may exhibit obsessions and compulsions related to food, as in Obsessive-Compulsive Dis-

Depression is a common side effect of anorexia. Conversely, many people with depression develop anorexia-like symptoms, making it hard for doctors to tell how to treat the patient.

order; or may be preoccupied with an imagined defect in bodily appearance, as in Body Dysmorphic Disorder. If the individual with anorexia nervosa has social fears that are limited to eating behavior alone, the diagnosis of Social Phobia should not be made, but social fears unrelated to eating behavior (e.g., excessive fear of speaking in public) may warrant an additional diagnosis of Social Phobia. Similarly, an additional diagnosis of Obsessive-Compulsive Disorder should be considered only if the individual exhibits obsessions and compulsions unrelated to food (e.g., an excessive fear of contamination), and an additional diagnosis of Body Dysmorphic Disorder should be considered only if the distortion is unrelated to body shape and size (e.g., preoccupation that one's nose is too big).

SEARCHING FOR PERFECTION

In 1989, rising star Christy Henrich was rated the number two female gymnast in the United States; she placed fourth in the uneven bars competition at the 1989 World Championships. That year also marked the beginning of her five-year battle with anorexia nervosa, a battle that ended in 1994 when she died of multiple organ failure. She weighed 47 pounds.

Christy had been viewed as a model gymnast by her peers, full of strength and determination, always trying to improve. Her coach, Al Fong, remembers her as extremely driven, a perfectionist, and impossible to deter from her chosen path. It was this quest for perfection, the attempt to force her maturing body to retain the girlish figure idealized in her sport, that drove Christy to begin to starve herself.

Girls who participate in prestigious levels of gymnastic competition often feel pressured to maintain rigid schedules of exercise, and to keep their bodies as thin as possible. Some coaches have been known to verbally abuse their charges, humiliating them for perceived fatness, and judges at the competitions sometimes tell girls

In the photo to the far left, taken in 1988, the 4-foot-10 Henrich weighed 93 pounds. She weighed 60 pounds in this 1993 photo taken with fiancé Bo Moreno.

they need to lose weight to compete more effectively. Until very recently, few coaches had enough understanding of nutrition or female development to be able to help the girls lose weight safely. In this kind of atmosphere, anorexia can become epidemic. Some studies have claimed that more than half of all girls involved in elite gymnastics have some form of eating disorder. The death of Christy Henrich, as well as gymnast Cathy Rigby's much-publicized battle with bulimia, have called attention to the seriousness of this problem.

Two teens look at diet cookbooks. Sometimes it is hard to tell where the diet ends and the eating disorder begins.

EXTREME DIETING: IS IT A DISORDER OR ONLY A DIET?

There can be a fine line between a diet and an eating disorder. Even in alarming cases in which signs of anorexia or bulimia are obvious in an individual, the diagnosis may be inconclusive. For example, a woman might have most of the symptoms of anorexia and appear to be grossly thin but still menstruate. Is she anorexic? Officially, no.

It has been estimated that most women in college indulge in at least one eating binge a year. One in five, according to that source, binges but may not purge at least once a week. Many of them aren't particularly worried about their weight and indeed don't need to be concerned (*Harvard*, Dec. 1992–Jan. 1993). These people are obviously neither bulimic nor anorexic.

But the complexity of the problem increases as the binging becomes more frequent. What if a person both binges and purges an average of, say, five times a month? Whereas this person does not meet the twice-a-week requirement for a bona fide bulimic diagnosis, he or she clearly has a problem. Some of these individuals would be placed in the category the *DSM-IV* designates as eating disorder not otherwise specified.

To further complicate the issue, as we have already seen, many anorexic and bulimic persons also exhibit depression. Conversely, an eating irregularity is one possible symptom of clinical depression. A person's eating disorder may therefore be regarded as a variation of depression (*Harvard*, Dec. 1992–Jan. 1993).

In order to make a correct diagnosis, an examiner must determine which symptom is stronger: Is the person a victim of depression, with side effects resembling anorexia? Or is the person an anorexic, with side effects resembling clinical depression? It's not always a clear call. A 1992 World Health Organization report suggests anorexia nervosa is an "independent syndrome" in a person if 1) "the clinical features of the syndrome are easily recognized, so that diagnosis is reliable with a high level of agreement between clinicians," and 2) the main features of anorexia nervosa are ongoing, or chronic.

Do coexisting disorders in a person aggravate each other? That is another issue researchers and doctors are studying. The *Harvard Medical School Mental Health Letter* reports that a woman who is "predisposed to depression may be more likely to develop an eating disorder if she goes on a strict diet" (Dec. 1992–Jan. 1993).

In our next chapter, we'll look at the suspected causes of anorexia nervosa.

An anorexic looking at herself in a mirror. Most anorexics are female, and the most common image of the anorexic is of the teenage girl.

5

CAUSES AND SPECIAL CONSIDERATIONS

P erhaps you have noticed that most of the anorexic individuals described thus far in this book had something in common: most were women or young girls. Not all people who suffer from anorexia nervosa or other eating disorders are female, but most are. Females may be 10 times more likely to develop eating disorders than males (Bowers and Andersen, 1995). Before we think about the possible reasons for this, it will be helpful to consider what is known about the underlying causes of anorexia.

EXPLANATION CAN BE DIFFICULT

In studying the disease, researchers often look closely at teenagers and preteens and at their family systems (which includes family customs, rules, and so forth). Lifestyle, upbringing, social environment, and other factors all seem to contribute to why some people develop anorexia nervosa. Doctors suspect experiences and notions that are developed during childhood lie near the root of eating disorders. But they also know that events later in life can raise questions about a person's identity and thus trigger anorexia nervosa (Gagnon, 1996). For other anorexics, doctors simply don't understand why they have the disorder. Certainly no one cause can be blamed for the disease.

What researchers do know is that many anorexics believe thinness is the key to happiness and success in life. They also tend to want everything in their lives to be perfectly ordered. Being in complete control of their weight is, to them, an important part of this overall life plan. For example, moving away from home for the first time, perhaps starting college or joining military service after high school graduation, brings the kind of stress that's sometimes associated with anorexia (*DSM-IV*). A broken relationship might

Doctors suspect that genetics play a role in anorexia. Close relatives of an anorexic are more likely to become anorexics themselves, or to develop other eating disorders.

be a factor; or, at the opposite extreme, marriage can trigger it.

GENETICS

At the same time, some researchers suspect heredity plays a role in the likelihood of a person developing the disorder. The *DSM-IV* says there is an "increased risk of anorexia nervosa among first-degree biological relatives of individuals with the disorder." One study of anorexic women indicates that 2 percent of the patients' sisters and mothers also had the disorder. Other research suggests the rate of anorexia among these first-degree relatives may be even higher (*Harvard*, Dec. 1992–Jan. 1993).

Among twins, there is evidence that anorexia nervosa is more likely to occur in both twins if the twins are monozygotic (identical) rather than dizygotic (fraternal) (*DSM-IV*). One study found that anorexia was evident in both siblings in 9 out of 16 cases of identical twins in which at least one of the twins was anorexic, while in only 1 out of 14 cases of fraternal twins (*Harvard*, Dec. 1992–Jan. 1993)

FAMILY PROBLEMS

Some psychiatrists see family situations as possible contributors to mental disorders. It could be that in some cases a young person's troubled behavior is, ironically, an attempt to restore normal family relationships. For example, if parents are alienated and seem to be on the verge of separation or divorce, their child may stop eating. The purpose seems to be to make both parents united in their concern about the child's health (*Harvard*, Dec. 1992–Jan. 1993).

A fear of growing up has also been suggested as a possible issue. The idea is that dieting or intentionally starving somehow enables the youth to remain a child longer.

Another theory is that the families of anorexics have strict rules and rigid expectations. In such a situations the children find it difficult to face the changes and challenges that come with entering the teen years. They find it especially hard to maintain healthy relationships and attitudes at this time (*Harvard*, Dec. 1992–Jan. 1993). According to one source, "Some children and teenagers seem to find that saying 'no' to food is the only way they can either express their feelings or have any influence in the family."

As we have seen, anorexics tend to be perfectionists who are highly stressed by criticism. Is this mind-set fostered by exceptionally high expectations by parents? Are the youths pressured to live up to outstanding performances by their sisters and brothers in schoolwork and athletics? If so, can these stiff demands contribute to anorexia nervosa? These are prevalent theories, and proving these theories is difficult. As the *Harvard Medical School Mental Health Letter* points out, "it is

Not all anorexics are female. The percentage of anorexics who are boys is small, but significant. Boys tend to have different motivations behind their eating disorders than girls.

unclear when the family causes the patient's problems and when the patient causes the family's".

Unreasonable expectations can also come from the person's friends and peers. Society puts a high value on an attractive figure. If the person feels unattractive—especially after dieting and exercising—he or she may feel like a failure. And failure, as we know, is a great fear of many anorexics. The person may then launch an even more severe weight control program. But no matter how much weight is lost, it won't be enough to satisfy the anorexic.

CHEMICAL IMBALANCES

Another factor researchers look for is the possibility of abnormal biological features in anorexics. For instance, some believe anorexics may suffer from imbalances in the production and regulation of hormones and of the neurotransmitters (brain chemicals) that affect a

A WEEK TO LIVE

In 1993, Marya Hornbacher checked into a hospital at age 18, weighing 52 pounds. Doctors said if she didn't start eating, she would be dead within a week. Faced with that drastic choice, Marya finally managed to start eating again, beginning to turn around her struggle with anorexia. She calls it the most difficult choice she ever made.

Marya had fought with bulimia from a very early age, and became anorexic at age 15. She was hospitalized at age 16, for the first of seven times. Like many anorexics, she equated starving herself with control, and equated that control with respect. The less she ate, she thought, the more "perfect" she could become. She could not have been more wrong.

As a result of Marya's years of struggle with eating disorders, her body has become severely damaged. Even now that she has put the worst of her anorexia behind her, the effects of her years of being malnourished will not disappear. Her bones are brittle, she has ulcers in the lining of her stomach and esophagus, her immune system is damaged, she may be permanently infertile, and her heartbeat is weak and erratic. And yet, she remains optimistic about her future.

Marya believes she is winning the battle with anorexia now; she has managed to find the strength within herself to fight the disease. She says she is no longer living for the mirror, in pursuit of unattainable thinness. She has written a book about her struggle called *Wasted: A Memoir of Anorexia and Bulimia*, based on a shorter work which won her the White Award for Best Freelance Story of 1993. Her struggle is not over; every day, she has to choose to eat. But she has survived, and each day it gets a little bit easier to make the choice to live.

person's appetite. Balance in a person's chemical makeup is vital for maintaining, among many other things, healthy weight and mood. Some investigators have suggested that chemical abnormalities in anorexics result in a form of addiction to fasting (*Harvard*, Dec. 1992–Jan. 1993).

Some research indicates anorexics possess low levels of norepinephrine, a neurotransmitter that affects, among other things, a person's mood and tolerance to stress. Anorexia may also be linked to problems with the part of the brain that controls metabolism.

The presence of chemical imbalances in parts of the brain that control both mood and appetite may help explain the relationship between depression and anorexia. But even if chemical imbalances can be conclusively proven, a critical question remains unanswered: Do biochemical problems cause anorexia nervosa, or do they result from the malnutrition that anorexics bring upon themselves?

ANOREXIA IN MALES

In a 16-year study, Oxford researchers compared male and female anorexics to see what differences, if any, existed in the symptoms and effects of the disorder between the men and women (Margo, 1987). The study revealed several differences.

For one, male anorexics tended to be abnormally concerned not so much with their weight as with their figure. Many of them actually were, or had been, a little "fat." The criticism (or perceived criticism) this can bring to a boy can have lasting effects. The distinction here is that while many male anorexics were combating actual obesity, females were more likely to be combating perceived obesity. Many female anorexics insisted they were fat even when they were dangerously thin. Another physical difference discovered between the males and the females is that many of the males were shorter than average, whereas the anorexic women tended to be a bit taller than average.

Another difference is that male anorexics were more involved in physical activities. Males more than females gave the desire to be more competitive in sports as a reason for their dieting.

In some teenage boys and young men, excessive dieting was seen as an attempt to prevent disease. For example, an anorexic teenage boy might live in fear that he'll have a heart attack, especially if family members have died of heart problems. His reasoning is that by keeping himself thin, he will help fend off the disease (Bowers and Andersen, 1995).

The physical differences between anorexic persons of the opposite sex are obvious. When anorexic women diet excessively, their menstrual cycles are usually interrupted very quickly. In anorexic men, on the other hand, the onset of sexual impotence is usually gradual.

Beyond these differences, researchers are not sure exactly how eating

Eating disorders seem to occur more in developed, Westernized countries, where food is abundant enough that self-starvation can be viewed as an act of self-discipline. One study has found that bulimia is also more common in cities than in rural areas.

disorders differ in males and females. Is alcohol or drug use more likely to accompany anorexia in men than in women? Are male anorexics more likely to be antisocial? The answers to these questions are inconclusive. According to one research report, "the general rule is that the more ill the person, the less the gender matters in treatment. Gender plays a significant role in treatment as weight becomes normal and binge-purge behaviors are interrupted" (Bowers and Andersen, 1995).

One thing that is known is that anorexia is less common in men than in women. The Oxford report previously cited observed: "Because men are both less subject to mood disorders and less concerned about body shape, they develop anorexia nervosa much less often" (Margo, 1987).

And because of this, male anorexia has not been studied as thoroughly. One survey of male college students, which was discussed in the *American Journal of Psychiatry*, found, among other things, that "childhood physical and sexual abuse appeared slightly more common" among men with eating disorders than among women. But generally, the characteristics of eating disorders among men and women are "strikingly similar." The study found no apparent link between homosexuality and male eating disorders. The journal report did suggest that eating disorders in males may be more widespread than medical records indicate. The reason is that "men with eating disorders are more reluctant than women to seek treatment" (Olivardia et al., 1995).

SOCIOECONOMIC FACTORS

Is anorexia a disease of the rich? Not necessarily, although many anorexics are well-to-do. For the most part, they are found in the United States, Europe, and other wealthy, industrially developed areas. The *Harvard Medical School Mental Health Letter* explains the reason for this: "Self-starvation cannot serve as a form of self-discipline unless the supply of food is abundant and reliable; most women in most places throughout history have not had that luxury." The report points out that "eating disorders are not simply a product of modern social conditions and the standards of body shape imposed by contemporary Western culture" (Dec. 1992–Jan. 1993). Interestingly, though, some researchers believe that people who emigrate from a country where anorexia is little known to a country where it is common "may develop anorexia nervosa as thin-body ideals are assimilated" (*DSM-IV*).

So while it's incorrect to call anorexia nervosa a "disease of the rich," the disorder does indeed appear to be found most commonly in developed countries. The Royal College of Psychiatrists observes: "In societies which do not value thinness, eating disorders are very rare. In surroundings such as ballet schools, where people value thinness extremely highly, they are very common."

An interesting study conducted in the Netherlands from 1985 to 1989 reviewed cases of anorexia nervosa and bulimia nervosa. The question was: does life in a large city, as opposed to a small community, affect the rate of these disorders? It was shown that, indeed, the per capita rate of bulimia was much higher in big cities. About 38 out of 100,000 females living in major cities in the Netherlands had bulimia, while fewer than seven out of 100,000 females living in the country suffered from the disorder. In contrast, "no rural-urban differences for anorexia nervosa" were discovered (Hoek et al., 1995).

AGE AS A FACTOR

Initial evidence seemed to indicate teenagers and young adults are more likely to develop anorexia nervosa than people in other age groups. Some researchers, though, believe the disorder is a very serious problem among older persons as well. In fact, certain evidence indicates anorexia can be more problematic among people in their later years. A report presented at the 1996 International Congress of Psychology indicates that young females account for only one-fifth of the actual deaths from anorexia and that most people who die as a result of the disorder are older than 45. According to one psychologist, "there has been a real bias in psychiatry and psychology, in terms of looking at people between the ages of 18 and 65. The phenomenon of disorders in our seniors is coming to people as a surprise" (Gagnon, 1996).

The percentage of males with the disorder seems to be higher among older adults than among young people. Even in that age group, though, the great majority of cases involve women (Gagnon, 1996).

A COMBINATION OF CAUSES

A 1992 report from the World Health Organization pointed to growing evidence that anorexia nervosa is caused by "interacting socio-cultural and biological factors." Understanding the relationships between the various factors is not easy. Analysts must ask such questions as, does a chemical imbalance lead to fasting, which leads to malnutrition, or does malnutrition cause the chemical imbalance to begin with? And to what extent might other factors be involved? These are the kinds of issues with which researchers struggle. A paper from the Royal College of Psychiatrists states: "There are many different ideas about the causes . . . and it is important to stress that not all will apply to every sufferer." We can see that the roots of anorexia nervosa are complex and are very likely interrelated.

Anorexia can be treated. In severe cases, where the patient has been battling the disease for years, hospitalization is often necessary at the beginning of treatment to help the patient begin to eat again.

6

TREATMENT

WHAT CAN BE DONE?

A norexic individuals should be encouraged, because there is much positive news in the battle to combat this disorder. The disease can be treated effectively, and the people it afflicts can live happy and productive lives. In their study of the disease, Dr. Wayne A. Bowers and Dr. Arnold E. Andersen report that "successful treatment of anorexia is a pragmatic blend of medical management, weight restoration, psychoeducational intervention, psychotherapy (individual, group, and family), and, at times, pharmacotherapy." ("Pharmacotherapy" is the medical term for using medicine to treat an illness.) Of course, as is true of most physical and/or mental illnesses, persons suffering from eating disorders have a better chance of long-term recovery if they receive early treatment. Individuals who seek help after years of dealing with the disorder are more likely to require repeated hospitalization (*Harvard*, Dec. 1992–Jan. 1993).

Notice that doctors carefully refer to the need for weight "restoration" as opposed to weight "gain." This is because to anorexics, of course, the idea of gaining weight is completely unacceptable.

An anorexic person's treatment team typically includes a psychiatrist, psychologist, specialist such as a gastroenterologist (a doctor who works with stomach/intestinal problems), dietary professional, social worker, occupational therapist, and nurse(s). Before treatment begins, doctors closely examine the patient's mental and physical condition. They record what the patient thinks about food and personal appearance. They look for signs of other disorders, particularly depression. They note physical details of the person's condition that might have resulted from the illness. They also consider any family history of similar problems.

If it is determined that treatment for anorexia nervosa is needed, it normally takes place on two levels. First is medical treatment, during which the anorexic, if the case is severe, is hospitalized. Second is psychosocial treatment, in which the therapists attempt to alter the person's attitude and behavior in regard to weight control.

Let's see what's involved in each.

MEDICAL TREATMENT

In certain cases, the anorexic person may be treated as an outpatient, living at home but checking in regularly with a doctor for treatment and evaluation. Outpatient care requires full cooperation and help from the person's family. However, if the disease is severe (for example, if the person frequently vomits as a method of weight control), outpatient treatment will likely be insufficient. The person will probably have to be hospitalized as treatment begins. Some anorexics are hospitalized for two to six months. Then, once they become outpatients, their monitoring and care may last for years.

Remember that the ultimate result of anorexia nervosa is death by starvation. So the first objective of the medical care phase is to ensure that doesn't happen. The individual must be adequately nourished before any form of long-term treatment can begin.

By the time some anorexics are admitted to a hospital, they are in an alarming condition. Their immediate plan of care may require drastic measures, such as tube feeding and total bed rest. The severely ill person may then have to start on a liquid diet and progress to a diet that begins at 1,500 to 2,000 calories a day and increases. Six balanced meal periods are recommended each day. Eventually, it is hoped the patient can receive from 3,500 to 5,000 calories a day, depending on the person's size. The medical staff must guard the patient closely following a meal to ensure the patient does not vomit; the bathroom is always off-limits to the patient immediately after a meal. The staff also monitors the patient's weight, regularly taking into account the consumption and output of fluids. Usually a weight gain of about a quarter pound a day represents good progress.

As the patient progresses by gaining weight, a system of rewards or privileges is implemented to allow the patient more freedom (Long, 1995–97). For example, whereas the doctor may have initially prescribed meals as a form of "medicine," over time the individual is

Princess Diana, whose struggle with an eating disorder was well-documented, meets the cast of the movie Haunted *at a premiere to aid the European Anorexia Trust. The charity was founded by Anthony Andrews (left), the film's star, after his daughter suffered from anorexia.*

allowed more and more control in choosing the kinds of food and the amounts—the total "energy intake"—to be prescribed (Bowers and Andersen, 1995). Other rewards in the hospital might include increased visiting privileges, social activities, and simply more freedom to leave the bed and move around.

Can medicine—a shot or a pill—restore an anorexic person to a "normal" state? No. No drug has been found to treat the overall illness directly. One researcher who examined studies of various medications used to treat anorexia nervosa reported that "many clinicians believe that medication does not significantly affect outcome" (Agras, 1995).

A teen visits her therapist. Psychotherapy for the patient is often a key component of recovery from anorexia.

However, certain types of medication can help relieve some of the symptoms of the disease, which can help the patient make progress in the long, difficult struggle. Doctors refer to medicine as an "adjunctive treatment" for anorexics; that is, medicine isn't the solution, but it can help.

One type of drug used in treating anorexia is an antidepressant. Relief from depression can help improve the person's eating behavior. One study has shown that dosages of a drug called methylphenidate seemed to alleviate anorexic symptoms in several elderly patients whose primary illness was severe dementia (Maletta and Winegarden, 1993). Other forms of medication prescribed for anorexics may include appetite stimulants, antipsychotics, and antihistamines.

In cases where depression is severe, doctors may recommend electroconvulsive therapy (ECT). This method of "shock treatment" has been used successfully to diminish depression for some people. Clearly, doctors cannot "shock" a person out of an anorexic state of mind. But if ECT can help control a patient's depression, it becomes one of many useful tools at the doctors' disposal.

PSYCHOSOCIAL TREATMENT

Treating anorexia is much more than forcing the patient to go through the motions of gaining weight. Unless therapists can establish in the anorexic a healthy attitude about weight and physical appearance, it will be only a matter of time before the person returns to starvation. It's not enough just to train the person to make "right" choices in regard to eating. Therapists must deal with why the person has negative associations with food. They must carefully teach the person the facts about nutrition and body weight.

Furthermore, they must explore with the patient the causes of the person's low self-esteem. Teenage girls, for example, may be anxious about schoolwork, boys, or family problems.

A therapist's first step is to earn the patient's confidence and cooperation. This is difficult because most anorexics do not want to be treated. They are convinced that looking emaciated really is beautiful and are skeptical when relatives, friends, or doctors tell them otherwise. When they arrive at a doctor's office, they've often been dragged there by friends or relatives. The therapist faces the formidable task of making an anorexic understand that his or her obsession with weight control is unreasonable and harmful. The therapist must make the person see a change is really needed (Long, 1995–97).

It's important that the individual truly understand he or she has a problem. Treatment does little good if the person fakes going along with the program only until he or she is released. Many anorexics, in fact, quickly plunge back into their old mind-set and within a few months or a year are alarmingly malnourished once more.

As suggested earlier, the family has a major role in treating anorexia, especially for younger persons. Family members must learn all about the disease and why their loved one acts the way he or she does. Ideally, the family must learn how, over time, to help the person recover gently, without constant arguments about eating habits.

Group therapy, too, can play a big role in treatment. Being with other anorexics and sharing stories can be an eye-opening experience. Among other things, it can make anorexics "see themselves in the mir-

A CLINIC'S TREATMENT OF ANOREXIA

Treatment of most severe cases of anorexia involves a stay in a hospital or clinic at the beginning of recovery. Rhodes Farm, a well-known clinic in London, treats children—mostly girls, although a few boys have been admitted—who are in the most severe state of anorexia, often too weak to climb stairs without assistance when they arrive and showing such signs of advanced anorexia as jaundiced skin and excessive body hair. Some talk of exercising until they faint from exhaustion, then waking up and beginning again. Many are close to death when they arrive.

The clinic combines therapy sessions with a child psychiatrist with regular, full

meals, a supervised exercise program, and day trips to help the children recover their enthusiasm for living. Patients are supervised to make sure they are not continuing their excessive exercise patterns or attempting to purge food while in the clinic. In rare cases, when patients refuse to give up their self-destructive habits, they may have to be placed under 24-hour supervision by the nurses. Usually, says clinic director Dr. Dee Dawson, "the threat of [24-hour supervision] is enough."

The long-term damage to their bodies may persist even after treatment: most of the girls have stopped menstruating long before they arrive at the farm, and they may have rendered themselves infertile, stunted their growth, and starved their bones of calcium, which can lead to a high risk of osteoporosis.

The clinic is pictured at left; teen anorexia patients share a communal meal above.

ror" like no other therapy can. Furthermore, it provides support from others who think much the same way and face the same problem.

CONTROLLING THE ILLNESS

An interesting project was reported by a team of doctors treating anorexic soldiers in the Israeli army (Mark et al. 1993). The soldiers found to be anorexic were typically women aged 18 to 20. As the doctors pointed out, "the army is a peculiar place for persons with anorexia nervosa." Army routine, with its vigorous daily exercise, is designed to keep a soldier's body and mind in excellent shape and his or her life in perfect order—which is just what most anorexics want. Indeed, anorexic symptoms (namely, a preoccupation with dieting and exercise) are hard for training officers to recognize among recruits because a controlled diet and exercise are basic parts of the army regimen.

At the same time, "the army requires women to abandon certain aspects of femininity and assume the identity of a soldier." Commanding officers prefer to see a soldier not as an individual but as a member of a unit. First names are dropped; individuals are known simply as Private plus their last name. For many new recruits (both men and women), this is a jarring blow to the ego and identity. This kind of situation can rush the disease to a crisis stage. Persons who enter military service with anorexic tendencies often experience a dramatic escalation of the problem.

Using negative reinforcement in their initial consultations with suspected anorexics, the Israeli doctors warned the soldiers they could be discharged from service if they refused treatment, which in Israel is a social stigma. More importantly, the doctors attempted to make clear the fact that the disease, if untreated, can lead to early death.

Most of the soldiers diagnosed with the disorder were admitted to an infirmary for four to six weeks. Then they were placed on a high-calorie diet. After each meal, the soldiers had to remain near a nurses' station for two hours. The reason: to discourage vomiting. If vomiting occurred in this public area, the offending patients were required to clean it up. Insensitive? No, necessary. The technique is in keeping with the caregivers' plan of psychotherapy. The doctors' objectives were to convince their patients they were malnourished and temporarily disturbed. They needed to "relearn regular eating habits."

Perhaps most important, the soldiers were taught the real meaning of self-control. Anorexics believe attaining and keeping a pencil-thin figure is visible proof they are in control of their bodies. To the contrary, the Israeli doctors strove to convince them their behavior was at best pseudocontrol and at worst self-destruction. The doctors' message: "Controlling the illness is the real mastery."

The doctors reported a happy ending for their study group: with medication and psychotherapy, three-fourths of the soldiers returned to full duty, and most of the others were able to resume limited duty.

But the doctors caution that mastering the illness does not happen easily or quickly. Doctors know they must correct both the physical problem of severe, deliberate malnutrition and the psychological problem that underlies this physical crisis. Drugs do not cure the illness, and persuading the anorexic to gain weight isn't enough either. The person must truly understand that a certain weight level is required for good health, that personal appearance is not the most important thing in life, and that "thin" is not necessarily "in"; in fact, it can be fatal.

REENTRY INTO A FOOD-MINDED SOCIETY

Sooner or later, caregivers hope to release the anorexic person back into the real world. They hope the individual will have acquired a positive, realistic attitude about bodily nourishment. They trust that the person will be able to make responsible, healthy choices about eating—without fear—on a daily basis.

This, of course, is the hard part. By comparison, restoring the person's weight and stamina in the hospital is a simple matter. Once released, the individual must determine whether his or her eating choices will be wise or will again lead to disaster. It is then that family encouragement and monitoring become especially important. They can observe the person ordering at restaurants and cooking at home. Is the individual concerned most with a balanced diet or with calorie counting?

By this point therapists have instructed the individual in preparing meals and in wise eating habits. Other therapists will have discussed proper forms of exercise. But ultimately, the matter is out of the hands of therapists. It is beyond the control even of family members and close friends. The anorexic individual will decide.

Unfortunately, therapists who deal with anorexia nervosa have come to expect that many of their patients will require hospitalization again in the future. Although some people experience symptoms of anorexia

CARALINE: A PORTRAIT OF DESPAIR

Caraline, a British woman who died of anorexia at the age of 29, did not become anorexic out of a wish to be thin, but as an expression of the pain and despair caused by parental sexual abuse when she was a child. Anorexia, in her case, was connected with a severe depression and her unhappiness at being alive. "My parents took away my soul," she wrote in her diary. "They stole my dignity. There is nothing left for me." Her overlapping problems with anorexia and depression underline the difficulty psychologists can face in determining what a person's primary disorder is, and how to most effectively treat him or her.

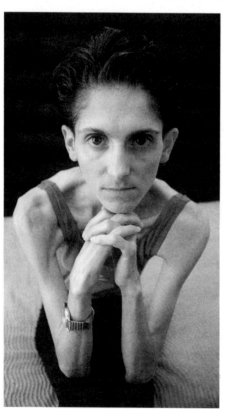

Caraline dedicated her brief life to explaining that eating disorders are not a product of girls' vanity, but a warning signal that something is wrong in their lives. The disorder, she said, is an outlet for them to show how much pain they are experiencing. She promoted counseling for anorexics, not force feeding. Simply forcing an anorexic to eat does nothing to help underlying psychological trauma such as Caraline suffered, and, she believed, can increase the patient's sense of helplessness or inadequacy.

Three eating-disorder self-help groups, as well as a memorial fund for anorexia treatment, have been established in England as a consequence of her story.

for a only few months (Rockwell, 1994), anorexia is generally regarded as a chronic disorder. With each repeated visit, doctors and staff know they won't fully cure the patient, but they hope to see progress in the long-term battle (*Harvard*, Dec. 1992–Jan. 1993).

Although anorexics can succeed in mastering their disorder and living productive lives, their basic personalities often remain unchanged. The *American Journal of Psychiatry* has reported that such characteristics as perfectionism and an abnormal concern with precision can be observed even after a "good outcome and recovery." That calls into question whether such traits really "contribute to the pathogenesis [origin and development] of this illness" (*American Journal of Psychiatry*, Nov. 1995).

In their 1995 article, Doctors Bowers and Andersen define the ultimate goal for the recovering anorexic as being able to "eat adequate amounts of a balanced variety of food in a normal manner with psychological and social comfort".

A painting made by an anorexic during the height of her illness, illustrating the depression and sense of withdrawal that many anorexics feel as their condition worsens.

RECOGNIZING THE DISEASE AND FINDING HELP

RECOGNIZING THE DISEASE IN SOMEONE ELSE

Most anorexics see no problem with their habits. When friends and relatives express concern about the anorexic's weight, he or she denies there is anything wrong. But there is something wrong. We have seen how the disorder can harm the person and eventually lead to death if it is not treated. In addition to the physical harm done, the individual can be grouchy and quick to anger and even become depressed and withdraw from friends and family. This kind of behavior affects not just the anorexic, but those who are close to him or her.

Perhaps you have a friend, brother, or sister whose strange eating behavior or physical condition makes you think he or she may have an eating disorder—perhaps anorexia nervosa. What should you do?

Watch carefully for warning signs. The obvious signals, as we have discussed, are drastic weight loss, fear of getting fat, and finding excuses not to eat. The person may also be preoccupied with exercising. Other possible symptoms are more subtle. The individual may be losing hair from the top of the head but growing more hair on the face or body. Room temperatures that others consider normal may make this person shiver. Because of sleeping irregularities, the person may appear tired in the middle of the day and have difficulty concentrating.

Of course, you must be careful not to jump to conclusions. Just because a person exhibits unusual hair growth or constantly feels chilly doesn't necessarily indicate anorexia. If a person yawns often and seems sluggish, he or she may not be getting enough regular sleep for reasons that have little or nothing to do with an eating disorder.

Anorexia can affect anyone. Some surveys have found a higher percentage of teenage and young adult females being treated for anorexia in recent decades.

Learn all you can about the disease. A counselor or doctor may be able to advise you how to raise and discuss the subject with the person. Of course, it is likely that the individual will deny there is a problem and even become defensive. Pose your questions and offer your observations gently and tactfully. Don't engage in an argument. Make it clear you merely want to be sure nothing is wrong and are there to support the person. Let your friend or relation know you are concerned about his or

WHO IS MOST AT RISK

n *The New Teenage Body Book*, Kathy McCoy names those most at risk for developing eating disorders. Girls are more vulnerable than boys. Topping the danger list:

1. Adolescent girls. Teen girls respond strongly to societal pressures to be thin and the normal emotional ups and downs of adolescence.

2. Perfectionists. Often excellent students, well-behaved and intent on doing everything right, including looking thin.

3. Members of weight-conscious families. Teens may try to please parents by becoming slim, or rebel by overeating.

4. Victims of early sexual traumas. Teen girls may unconsciously try to make their bodies unattractive to protect themselves against men.

5. Teens with low self-image. These young people are especially sensitive to suggestions they are overweight.

Source: *USA Today*

her happiness and well-being.

If your concern is ignored and the person continues to lose weight, bear in mind you are not bound by friendship to be silent. If the person is a friend, you should discuss your concern with his or her parents or other relatives. If the individual is a sister or brother, insist that he or she consult a doctor.

Although anorexics resist treatment and may be angered by friends and relations who try to help them, they nevertheless need to be cared for. They need to know someone is trying to understand them. The American Academy of Family Physicians stresses that "the most important thing that family and friends can do to help a person with anorexia is to love them."

And you must be patient. One thing that is fairly certain about anorexics is that the person's eating habits and beliefs about weight control will not change abruptly. If he or she truly is anorexic, you can expect a rocky recovery process that could take months or years. Periods of stabilization may be followed by relapses.

WHAT IF THE PERSON MIGHT BE . . . ME?

Find help. In rare cases, anorexics are able to recognize their disorder; correct their misconceptions about eating, physical appearance, and self-worth; and put themselves on a sensible diet. But for most people with the disorder, professional help is required.

If you see yourself in a debilitating cycle of fasting, weakness, and depression, don't be afraid to acknowledge you have a problem. Know that all the people around you—even the most attractive—have problems of their own. Their problems may be different from yours and may be invisible to the public eye, but they exist and need to be confronted, just as yours do.

Are you unhappy with yourself, even after diligent, dramatic attempts at weight control? Then weight control may not be the key to happiness, after all. Often, our greatest victories in life are simple admissions that we can never be in complete control. Once we admit that, we suddenly find ourselves free to get the help we need in order to really improve ourselves.

AN INCREASING PROBLEM?

Is anorexia nervosa becoming more commonplace in America and other countries? Not according to some research. For example, records from the Mayo Clinic showed no change in the overall rate of anorexia among a Minnesota city's population over a 45-year period. Other sources, however, indicate that the disorder may be increasing in frequency. Some surveys have found that in recent decades, a higher percentage of teenage and young adult females have been treated for anorexia (*Harvard*, Dec. 1992–Jan. 1993).

The difficulty in determining this frequency is due to the differing standards used in reporting the disorder. Whereas "the label 'anorexia nervosa' has often been used for any unexplained weight loss or aversion to food," notes the *Harvard Medical School Mental Health Letter*,

Anorexia remains a significant problem, even though treatment seems to be improving. Too often, young people create unhealthy standards for themselves, trying to emulate actors or fashion models who tend to be underweight. Convincing them that this is an unrealistic goal is a problem that remains to be solved.

some research casts out cases in which "the condition was too mild to deserve the name," or in which anorexialike symptoms may have been attributed to other causes. At the same time, other people's medical records may not mention the term "anorexia nervosa," even though the disease eventually is diagnosed in those individuals (*Mayo Clinic Proceedings*, 1988).

It could be that anorexia seems to occur more frequently because the disease has been brought to the public's attention more frequently in recent years (*Harvard,* Dec. 1992–Jan. 1993).

A study conducted among college students between 1982 and 1992 offers hope that Americans may be increasingly aware of the dangers of radical dieting. In this study, students were surveyed and categorized as 1) nondieters, 2) dieters with no apparent related problems, 3) problem dieters, 4) persons with eating disorders that did not demand clinical care, and 5) persons with medically definable eatable disorders. Over the 10-year period, researchers noted "significant reductions of problematic eating behaviors and disordered attitudes about body, weight, and shape." They observed significant reductions in the rates of bulimia nervosa, binge eating, and related symptoms.

The female students surveyed in 1992 were an average of 5 pounds heavier than those surveyed in 1982, and there was a greater tendency to be overweight. However, the researchers pointed to an overall "improved body image" and "healthier eating habits in terms of dietary intake and meal regularity."

They said the study suggests an apparent reduction in "problematic eating behaviors and eating disorder symptoms. . . . However, they remain a significant problem that affects a substantial segment of this population" (Heatherton et al., 1995).

FREEING SOCIETY OF THE DISORDER

Studies of anorexia nervosa have taught us much about the disease, but they are inconclusive and often flawed. Continuing research is needed. Investigators especially need more data from long-term anorexia study projects and from studies that examine anorexia's possible relationship to other psychological disorders (*Harvard,* Dec. 1992–Jan. 1993).

In the meantime, individuals and society as a whole need to examine carefully our culture's peculiar value system. No one questions the general need for healthiness. Exercise is vital. Sensible eating is too. But is your body supposed to look like the models' and actors' you see in movies, and television, and advertisements? Is that what it will take to make you successful and acceptable to others? Think carefully about that.

True success does not demand a "perfect" body, and true friends won't care whether or not you meet some impossible standard of beauty. One public awareness campaign states, "There are three billion women who don't look like supermodels, and only eight who do." It is perfectly possible to live a happy, successful life that does not depend on thinness. Redefining society's attitude about weight and physique begins with you. Don't judge people by their physical appearance—look at the things they can do, not the shapes of their bodies. And treat yourself the same way!

APPENDIX

FOR MORE INFORMATION

The following national organizations are dedicated to increasing awareness of anorexia nervosa and related eating disorders, and providing information to people with eating disorders who are trying to get help and recover.

American Anorexia/Bulimia Association, Inc.
165 West 46th St. #1108
New York, NY 10036
(212) 575-6200

**Eating Disorders Awareness
and Prevention, Inc.**
603 Stewart St., Suite 803
Seattle, WA 98101
(206) 382-3587

FED (Freedom from Eating Disorders)
14707 SW Parmele Rd.
Gaston, OR 97119
(503) 628-8027

**National Association of Anorexia Nervosa
and Associated Disorders, Inc.**
P.O. Box 7
Highland Park, IL 60035
(847) 433-4632

National Eating Disorders Organization
6655 S. Yale Ave.
Tulsa, OK 74136
(918) 481-4044

APPENDIX

SOURCES CITED

Agras, W. Stewart. "Treatment of Eating Disorders." In *American Psychiatric Press Textbook of Psychopharmacology*. Washington, D.C.: American Psychiatric Press, 1995.

Agras, W. Stewart, and Robert Berkowitz. "Behavior Therapy." In *American Psychiatric Press Textbook of Psychiatry*, 2nd edition. Washington, D.C.: American Psychiatric Press, 1994.

American Academy of Family Physicians [on-line]. Available at www.aafp.org.

American Psychiatric Association. *Diagnostic and Statistical Manual of Mental Disorders*, 4th edition. Washington, D.C.: American Psychiatric Press, 1994.

"Anorexia Nervosa in Rochester, Minnesota: A 45-Year Study." *In Mayo Clinic Proceedings* 63 (May 1988). Reprinted in *Internet Mental Health* [on-line]. Available at www.mentalhealth.com.

Bowers, Wayne A., and Arnold E. Andersen."Inpatient Treatment of Anorexia Nervosa." In *Treatments of Psychiatric Disorders*, 2nd edition. 2 vols. Washington, D.C.: American Psychiatric Press, 1995.

Casper, Regina C. "Biology of Eating Disorders." In *American Psychiatric Press Textbook of Psychopharmacology*. Washington, D.C.: American Psychiatric Press, 1995.

Dare, Christopher. "Psychoanalytic Psychotherapy." In *Treatments of Psychiatric Disorders*, 2nd edition. 2 vols. Washington, D.C.: American Psychiatric Press, 1995.

"Eating Disorders." In *The Harvard Medical School Mental Health Letter*. December 1992–January 1993.

Gagnon, Louise. "Despite Image, Most Anorexics Are 45 or Older." In *The Medical Post*, October 8, 1996. Reprinted in *Internet Mental Health* [on-line]. Available at www.mentalhealth.com.

Heatherton, Todd F., Patricia Nichols, Fary Mahamedi, and Pamela Keel. "Body Weight, Dieting, and Eating Disorder Symptoms Among College Students, 1982 to 1992." In *American Journal of Psychiatry* 152, no. 11 (November 1995).

Hoek, Hans W., Aad I. M. Bartelds, Jacquoline J. F. Bosveld, Yolanda van der Graaf, Veronique E. L. Limpens, Margo Maiwald, Caroline J. K. Spaaij. "Impact of Urbanization on Detection Rates of Eating Disorders." In *American Journal of Psychiatry* 152, no. 9 (September 1995).

Hsu, L. K. George, and Sing Lee. "Is Weight Phobia Always Necessary for a Diagnosis of Anorexia Nervosa?" In *American Journal of Psychiatry* 150, no. 10 (October 1993).

Lai, Kelly Y. C., Alfred H. T. Pang, and C. K. Wong. "Case Study: Early-Onset Anorexia Nervosa in a Chinese Boy." In *Journal of the American Academy of Child and Adolescent Psychiatry* 34, no. 3 (March 1995).

Long, Phillip W. (© 1995-1997). *Internet Mental Health* [on-line]. Available at www.mentalhealth.com.

Lucas, Alexander R., C. Mary Beard, W. Michael O' Fallon, and Leonard T. Kurland. "Is Anorexia Nervosa Becoming More Common?" *The Harvard Medical School Mental Health Letter*, September 1988.

Maletta, Gabe J., and Thomas Winegarden. "Reversal of Anorexia by Methylphenidate in Apathetic, Severely Demented Nursing Home Patients." In *American Journal of Geriatric Psychiatry* 1, no. 3.

Margo, J. L. "Anorexia Nervosa in Males: A Comparison with Female Patients." In *British Journal of Psychiatry* 151 (July 1987). Reprinted in *Internet Mental Health* [on-line]. Available at: www.mentalhealth.com.

Mark, Mordechai, Jonathan Rabinowitz, Stanley Rabinowitz, Bracha Gaoni, Isak Babur, and Yehuda L. Danon. "Brief Treatment of Anorexia Nervosa in Military Personnel." In *Psychiatric Services* 44, no. 1 (January 1993).

Olivardia, Roberto, Harrison G. Pope, Barbara Mangweth, and James I. Hudson. "Eating Disorders in College Men." In *American Journal of Psychiatry* 152, no. 9 (September 1995).

"Persistent Perfectionism, Symmetry, and Exactness After Long-Term Recovery from Anorexia Nervosa." In *American Journal of Psychiatry* 152, no. 11 (November 1995).

"Princess Margaret of Hungary." In *American Journal of Psychiatry* 151, no. 8 (August 1994).

Royal College of Psychiatrists, Leaflet reprinted by the Computers in
    Psychiatry Special Interest Group and Department of Mental Health,
    University of Exeter [on-line].
    Available at www.ex.ac.uk/cimh/help/help.htm.

Sullivan, Patrick F. "Mortality in Anorexia Nervosa." In *American Journal of
    Psychiatry* 152, no. 7 (July 1995).

World Health Organization, "Anorexia Nervosa: European Description." In
    ICD-10 Classification of Mental and Behavioural Disorders, Geneva (1992).
    Reprinted in *Internet Mental Health* [on-line].
    Available at www.mentalhealth.com.

APPENDIX

FURTHER READING

American Psychiatric Association. *Diagnostic and Statistical Manual of Mental Disorders*, 4th edition. Washington, D.C.: American Psychiatric Press, 1994.

———. *Treatment of Psychiatric Disorders*, 2nd edition. 2 vols. Washington, D.C.: American Psychiatric Press, 1994.

Apostolides, Marianne. *Inner Hunger: A Young Woman's Struggle Through Anorexia and Bulimia.* New York: W.W. Norton & Company, 1998.

Buckroyd, Julia. *Anorexia and Bulimia: Your Questions Answered.* Rockport, Mass.: Element Books Ltd., 1996

Epling, W. Frank, and W. David Pierce. *Solving the Anorexia Puzzle: A Scientific Approach.* Kirkland, Wash.: Hogrefe & Huber Publications, 1991.

Epstein, Rachel. *Eating Habits and Disorders.* Philadelphia: Chelsea House Publishers, 1990.

Hornbacher, Marya. *Wasted: A Memoir of Anorexia and Bulimia.* New York: HarperCollins, 1998.

Palmer, R.L. *Anorexia Nervosa: A Guide for Sufferers and Their Families.* New York: Penguin, 1989.

Sandbeck, Terrence J. *The Deadly Diet: Recovering from Anorexia and Bulimia* (2nd ed.) Oakland, Calif.: New Harbinger Publications Inc., 1993.

Sargent, Judy Tam. *The Long Road Back, A Survivor's Guide to Anorexia.* Saint Cloud, Minn.: North Star Press, 1998.

Vandereycken, Walter, and Ron Van Deth. *From Fasting Saints to Anorexic Girls: The History of Self-Starvation.* New York: New York University Press, 1994.

APPENDIX

GLOSSARY

Amenorrhea: the lack, or cessation, of a woman's menstrual periods due to extreme malnutrition.

Anemia: a condition in which a person does not have enough red blood cells, typically because of an iron deficiency.

Anorexia nervosa: an eating disorder in which a person eats as little as possible, and sometimes over-exercises or engages in purging behavior such as forced vomiting, because of an intense and unhealthy desire to lose weight.

Binging and purging: the practice, usually found in bulimics but occasionally in anorexics as well, of eating a very large amount of food at one time and then vomiting or abusing laxatives in an attempt to keep the body from processing the food.

Bulimia nervosa: an eating disorder characterized by frequent episodes (at least two per week) of binging and purging behavior.

Eating disorder: a psychological disorder in which a person is unable or unwilling to maintain normal eating habits, and instead engages in self-starvation, binging, purging, or some combination of these behaviors.

Electroconvulsive therapy: therapy consisting of a carefully controlled series of electric shocks, used to treat extreme cases of depression.

Gastroenterologist: a doctor who specializes in diseases and disorders of the stomach and digestive tract.

Neurotransmitter: a chemical in the brain that transmits signals, such as the need to eat or the feeling of pain.

Norepinephrine: a neurotransmitter that affects a person's mood and tolerance of stress. Some research has shown anorexics to have low levels of norepinephrine.

Pharmacotherapy: the technical term for using medicine to treat an illness or disorder. Antidepressants are sometimes used in the treatment of anorexia, since many anorexics also suffer from depression.

APPENDIX

INDEX

APPENDIX

PICTURE CREDITS

Senior Consulting Editor Carol C. Nadelson, M.D., is president and chief executive officer of the American Psychiatric Press, Inc., staff physician at Cambridge Hospital, and Clinical Professor of Psychiatry at Harvard Medical School. In addition to her work with the American Psychiatric Association, which she served as vice president in 1981-83 and president in 1985-86, Dr. Nadelson has been actively involved in other major psychiatric organizations, including the Group for the Advancement of Psychiatry, the American College of Psychiatrists, the Association for Academic Psychiatry, the American Association of Directors of Psychiatric Residency Training Programs, the American Psychosomatic Society, and the American College of Mental Health Administrators. In addition, she has been a consultant to the Psychiatric Education Branch of the National Institute of Mental Health and has served on the editorial boards of several journals. Doctor Nadelson has received many awards, including the Gold Medal Award for significant and ongoing contributions in the field of psychiatry, the Elizabeth Blackwell Award for contributions to the causes of women in medicine, and the Distinguished Service Award from the American College of Psychiatrists for outstanding achievements and leadership in the field of psychiatry.

Consulting Editor Claire E. Reinburg, M.A., is editorial director of the American Psychiatric Press, Inc., which publishes about 60 new books and six journals a year. She is a graduate of Georgetown University in Washington, D.C., where she earned bachelor of arts and master of arts degrees in English. She is a member of the Council of Biology Editors, the Women's National Book Association, the Society for Scholarly Publishing, and Washington Book Publishers.

Dan Harmon is a freelance editor and writer living in Spartanburg, South Carolina. He has written several books on humor and history, and has contributed historical and cultural articles to the *New York Times, Music Journal, Nautilus,* and many other periodicals. He is the managing editor of *Sandlapper: The Magazine of South Carolina* and is editor of *The Lawyer's PC* newsletter.